MW00931079

dear you

Love, Tiana Monique

Copyright © 2020 Tiana Monique Harrington

All rights reserved. No part of this book may be reproduced or used in any manner without written permission of the copyright owner except for the use of quotations in a book review. For more information, address: tianam.harrington@gmail.com

FIRST EDITION

Book cover by Anamaria Stefan
Typesetting and Interior Book Design by Anamaria Stefan
Illustrations by Anamaria Stefan

Dedication

For my family who have always loved me and my friends
who have always supported me.

you know who you are.

one.

'It's just like the water. I ain't felt this way in years.'

-Lauryn Hill

If you ever hear a song and think to yourself
'I wonder if when she hears this, she thinks of me...'

I do.
I always do.

| 'stick figures'

Immortalized on paper.
I remember those kids.
Broken and bent.
Scribbled and sloppy.
Colorless and confused.
I remember
Drawing happily ever after's
With invisible ink.
A hollow head
With no room to think.
Just kids.
Coloring outside of the lines.
Breaking the rules
One heart at a time.
You remember.
We were so young.
In love and elementary.
And now we're nothing
But stick figures
In a sweet memory.

'last words'

Just in case the last words I say to you are bitter,
Or if our last encounter with each other
Ends in distant stares.
In case we exchange words without
Thinking before speaking them.
In case your heart drops when you see me.
In case your eyes swell when you hear my name,
Remembering the hurt that I might place on your frame.
If I leave and the words I said to you
Fall beneath your breath, leaving you speechless.
In case you walk away believing you're alone,
Please know you brought a light to my life
That will never cease to burn bright.
Know that your name is embedded in my skin.
Know I loved you beyond measure.
In case we never speak again,
Please know you were the muse
That kept my ordinary words singing.

'the boy I used to write poems about'

The boy I used to write poetry about
Shows up with words spilling out of his pockets.
He cannot speak and
Can only hear melodies.
The boy I used to write poems about,
Has a heart beating outside of his chest.
He bleeds ink.
The boy I used to write poems about
Is made out of paper.
He is terrified of matches.
The boy I used to write poems about
Is a prisoner of notebooks kept on dusty shelves.
The boy I used to write poems about
Has a spine shaped like a question mark.
He smells like a library.
The boy I used to write poems about
Never asked to read them.
So I locked him away in a cursive memory.
If you ask him, he'll tell you I left him for dead.
But I left him in this poem, instead.

Your kiss tastes like
Infinity signs dipped in merlot.
It takes like overcast mornings.
And warm coffee.
Your kiss feels like vinyl
Spinning on my tongue.
Your kiss feels like
Pulling my favorite sweater out of the dryer
On the coldest winter night.
Your kiss is the purest water.
Your kiss is the strongest whiskey.
Now kiss me
Until
I
Drown.

You did not love me and that's okay.
You did not stay and that is fine.
You were not honest and even that
Is forgivable.
But what I cannot wrap my head around,
The concept that I cannot seem to grasp
Is the fact that you took it upon yourself to
Make it seem like all of this
Was somehow my fault.
As if I asked you
Not to love me,
To leave,
Or to lie.
You wanted so badly
For your image to remain untouched
That you tried to kill me to keep your
Innocence alive.
How quickly you forgot
That you cannot shoot me
With my own bullets.
Lost souls never win.
And you will sink in the waters
You've decided to swim within.
But I am fully prepared to watch you go down.
And it's not because you did not love me.
And it's not because you wanted to leave
And it's not because you refused to tell the truth.
It is because and simply
When this ends,
I will be strong enough to stand here
Wrapped entirely in all the love that you did not want
And listen to you beg for the name
That you did not defend.

You see,
He was everything I wanted, *until he wasn't.*

But I will not reminisce on days that never came.
I will not replay memories that never happened,
And I will never wish they had.
Moments come when they are supposed to,
Never rushing and never late
Though I crave you still;
I will not indulge in your
Yesterday.

'threads'

It was like watching sheets unravel
The way our hands left each other.
We used to be close, like sleeping eyelids.
Confined in the warm embrace
Your breath sent to the creases in my neck.
We were facts.
But we could never find our truth, so our hands parted.
Those pretty hands with psalms written in stone.
They were too heavy for me to carry so I let go.
Hoping that one day you would shake that weight off
And we could be featherlike again.

'*this is how I breathe*'

I inhale your existence.
I exhale your absence.
I breathe your memory.

inhale
iloveyou.
exhale
Imissyou.

And then it's quiet.

'untitled I'

I know that I need to accept the fact that I can't keep you
forever, but selfishly I keep your memory in queue.
And when they ask me for my name I attach it to your last, not
because I miss you, but because time is moving too fast, and
I'm just trying to capture the history
before it becomes the past.

'puzzle pieces'

I can't keep doing this.
I can't keep relearning how to love you.
I can't keep breaking off pieces of my heart,
Expecting you to finish the puzzle.
The picture has always been you,
But I can't fix this.
You keep giving me corner pieces,
But refuse to let me figure out who is inside.
You are the frame, let me fill you.
Every time you walk away, I try to heal you.
But I have wounds too.
I tend to yours, and tend to forget that
I am still
Undone.
So, I'm emptying the box on the table.
I'm spreading out the broken pieces of us.
And you're going to stay,
And finish this.
For good this time.

'the truth we're avoiding'

We are going through the motions,
But we're not moving.
We're saying words,
But we're not speaking.
We're doing everything
We think we should do.
And nothing that we need to.

And maybe we're too afraid to admit
What that really means.

While walking past a mirror,
I saw your sweet reflection.
I ran and hugged you until the glass
s h a t t e r e d
Into my arms,
Your memory bleeding down to my fingertips.
I tend to kiss the scars when I begin to forget
Your smile.

I re-read a poem I once wrote you
And it brought me to tears.
Not because of the words I wrote,
But because of the words you never asked to hear.

'eight minutes'

I spent eight minutes writing
Your name
In cursive
Until my pen bled
And the pages began to
Dampen with tears
And the edges turned black and curled over
With the burn
Of each memory
Lost.
I spent eight minutes writing
Your name
In cursive
Cramping my wrist
With each stroke.
Your name is beautiful
In cursive
In print.
Infinite.
Signing each line with
A poetic flame.
Your name was carried
With the scent of summer
And the page blossomed with
Daisies and roses.
I spent eight minutes writing
Your name
In cursive
Before I realized
I had started writing mine.

I wish I could flip myself inside out
So you could see the decayed lyrics
Written on my rib cage.
Wish I could play you the
Melodies of this broken heart.
It would sound like
Coltrane's, In a Sentimental Mood
Chopped and screwed and
Backwards.
I wish I could magnify my palms
To make you realize how short my lifeline
Really is and maybe then you'd understand
Why I refuse to deal with this bullshit.
Maybe if I could put my tears in
An hour glass, I could possibly
Turn back the hands of time,
And you could listen to my cry
Over and over.

This is a never-ending war.
Between you and my common sense.
Between me and your judgement.
Between us and the concept of love.
We never really knew what is was,
So we just went.
Never yielded at the signs that
Told us to slow down.
Never stopped at the red lights.
And look where we ended up.
Alone and lost.

'do not enter'

I could feel you
Trying to break in
Trying to unlock the passwords,
Scrambling for the key
In deserted memories.
I heard you knocking
But the door knob
Burst into flames when
I went to let you in.

'Shakespeare lied'

Please do not romanticize the idea of me.
I am no love lost.
This is not a Shakespeare tragedy.
Far from lover's star crossed.
Do not glorify the toxicity.
Do not beautify the complicity.
Please do not look back and try to
Simplify the complexities.
It was never written in our destinies.
And though at times, I find myself
Longing for those small moments of bliss
I know we were never meant to be.
Once upon a time, I thought maybe
We could defy the stars.
But I stopped hanging off of balconies
When you left too many scars.
You are no Montague.
I am no Capulet.
Though you may be fortune's fool,
I am not your Juliet.

If you asked me what poetry tasted like, I'd say you.

When I look back I realize
There were so many times
When I loved you
And I should've hated you.

I hope that when you look back you realize
All those times
You tried to hate me
You should've loved me.

Someday I'll forget you.
Maybe not completely.
But eventually
I'll awake with dry eyes.
And your absence won't be so heavy.
Someday, and it may not be soon, but someday
I'll walk hand in hand with someone new
And mean it.
I'll start to forget what your smile looks like
Or the shape of your eyes
Or how they change color in the morning.
Your scent will begin to fade from my pillows
And my notebook pages will stop
Mourning for your name.
I'll no longer reminisce on what
We could have been.
I'll stop writing for you.

Someday.
Maybe.
But not
Today.

In case you are looking for me,
I left clues in your memory.
I was the calligraphy written
On emerald stones, sending letters
To the angels that carried your spirit.
I was the cracks in the sidewalk that
You avoided because of superstitions.
The babies cry in crowded rooms.
The emptiness that filled
Eternity; the definition of your
Nightmares.
I was always in plain view before
You began looking for me.
I've always been here.
I was always there,
But you never saw, never needed to search
For what was in front of you, my love.
Isn't that how it goes?

There was that one time
When I cried and I
Shed tears of merlot.
You watched me ignite into
My purest form.
I poured every drop of love
I had left into your lap
Like you were an empty wine glass.
I filled you to the brim with
Words I could have never said sober
And all you could say was
That I drank too much.
And I remember you trying to hold me and laughing.
Your hands on the small of my back.
You made me feel like a child
And I hated you for that.
For thinking you were my shelter.
I needed you to love me.
But you left me destroyed.
Broken, like wine bottles on wooden floors.
And because of you I now know
That you cannot confide in a hurricane
And you cannot seek comfort in the
Arms of a tornado.

You can keep holding on if you want to,
But *nothing* is a silly thing to want to keep.

And it wasn't that I didn't have the beauty.
And it wasn't that I wasn't smart enough.
And it wasn't that we didn't have the chemistry.
You were just lost.
And me thinking I was your destination
Is where the road stopped.
You traveled distances in search of your happiness.
When in reality
I could've shown you the way
If you would've just let me.
But you went astray
And found yourself a home in the unknown.
A place where I cannot follow.
A place where my name is erased.
A place where you are not mine.
And I hope someday
In another life maybe
You find your way back to forever.
Because we almost had it this time,
Didn't we?

Don't bother me with words.

I have enough of those.

You keep saying

And explaining

But I just want you to feel.

I want you

To collapse in the silence.

I want you to surrender to this moment

Where dictionaries are foreign objects.

And poems are silenced.

The only words I want to read

Are the ones your fingers

Write in cursive along the arch of my back.

All I want to hear

Is the sound of your exhale

Bouncing off my skin.

This has nothing to do with words, love.

And I know that's hard sometimes,

To try and not analyze this,

But love has no logic.

It has no sense to be made

Or any reasonable reasons.

It just is.

And there are no words for that.

'*roses & thorns*'

I told a man I once loved
That I hated flowers.
And what bothered me the most
Wasn't the fact that I had lied,
But because I
Felt that I had to.
He was cold.
And I found myself wanting to hide
Any soft part of me.
What I did not realize was that I had
Given him an excuse to not treat me sweetly.
Instead I got salt poured into wounds
He continued to open
Over and over again.
I gave him a reason to be lazy
With the love I was all too willing to give.
In turn, this became the root to me thinking
I did not deserve love.
And for years I punished myself for it.
Do not let yourself be silenced.
You voice is the most powerful weapon
You will ever have.
Never let anyone take that away from you.
And always always always
Demand flowers.

If you can't hear my silence,
How can I trust you with my words?

'dear you'

It doesn't look like a lot but
This is all I have.
I write you love letters
Because words are the most
Valuable things I own
And you're the only one
I want to give them to.

'woman with words I'

Hearts jump off bridges every day.
And they never televise these suicides
But why can't I publicize the
Mass genocide of my insides?
I heard love cries in the dark and then falls apart.
They never tell us that love murders the heart.

Licking wounds with razor blades.
Muted tongues play heartbeats like drums.
Souls strung together with cold wire,
Words are left unsung and deferring
In the blazing sun.
Days fall into the middle of my lap and
Nights are drowned in the sound of tears
Caressing damp pillows.
Grey skies kiss happiness goodbye,
Lips painting bleak lullabies.
Humming into me these sweet soliloquies
And he left me
Without
Warning.

Salt
Pouring
Into fresh cut pores.
Wrapping burnt fingertips from touching
Unwelcomed realms
I know I should have known better.
Monday's moon collapses
And tomorrows come too soon.
This is where sorrow becomes my muse.
Falling backwards into green stones
I resort to comfort zones.
Loneliness creeps underneath doorways
And snakes up my legs to find a home
In the dimples of my cheeks.
She fed him warm words while mine

Sent a painful chill down his back
Which, is why her name echoes
After he says "love".

And I am left, twisting my arm
To make sure I am still human.
Delicate spirits broken with glass
The shattered pieces falling among my eyes lids
I never saw it coming.
Arms wrapping around active thoughts to remain
Balanced and sane
Catching my breath in the heat of the moment
Apple colored kisses keeping me hostage,
We lost it.
And I'm exhausted from dodging bullets
To protect my heart
And following trails only to find
Question marks at the end of the tunnel.

The distance makes the difference
Between me and his mistress
And I guess I didn't listen when the winds hissed
That his lips kissed a new miss
And honestly I don't give a fuck about your misery, no diss.
Because you took away the only image I had left of bliss.
So with this, I claim victim.
Pretending to not feel how bad
The realization of it burns.
I guess this is how karma works.

He always did love a woman with words.

I hate that I still think of you when I write poetry.
I hate that your name is written
In sloppy cursive on every page.
That your smile is embedded in every simile,
That every finished chapter, ends with your memory.
I hate that I still think of you
As poetry.

I will not lie.
You have not escaped my thoughts
Since you entered them.
It's true.

You remind me of Lauryn Hill lyrics.

two.

'look,
Don't we make
beautiful victims?'

-Saul Williams

'Darling'

I'd drive up narrow mountains for you.

Throw pennies into fountains for you.

I'd sleep in run down motels for you.

Smoke L's on the rooftop of SF hotels for you.

Wipe away your tears for you.

My nigga, I'd do years for you.

I'd stay quiet even if I was afraid for you.

So many times, I've fallen to my knees and prayed for you.

I'd go fast for you.

Flee the scene when we crash for you.

Put money on my phone for you.

Show up to court to show you're not alone for you.

Write love letters for you.

I'd be better for you.

Kiss all your scars for you.

Love from afar for you.

Forget what we had for you.

If I could, I'd undo the past for you.

Because I still have love for you,

Even if that's not enough for you.

My love, I will for you.

My dear, I did for you.

'royals'

You are as much a king now
As you were when we met.
I could tell the moment
Your Midas hand turned my thoughts
Into gold thread.
With your Zeus like stature
You captured me
In a way that only a god could.
Blue blooded, though
You saw me as peasant.
Using pawns to
Make me fall in love.
You took it as weakness,
Playing chess with my heart
While I protected your kingdom.
You let us fall apart,
Your love left me bleeding.
Treated you like royalty
Abusing my loyalty.
Failing to understand
You were the very soul of me.
My crown shone bright, but you were
Blinded by women who
Posed on fake thrones.
Oblivious to the poison they held
Underneath their pretty clothes.
We could have ruled the world.
I told you to choose
Which meant letting you lose me.
I am as much a queen now as
I was when we met.

It's a shame you did not see.

'charlie buckets'

Sometimes it takes hitting rock bottom,
To appreciate a view.
I look at you and see oceans.
I see sunsets and waterfalls.
You live in a world I never thought existed.
A world filled with magic and chocolate covered kisses.
And it wasn't like I went looking for it.
All I wanted was to be loved,
And you were my golden ticket.
And I'll die with you
Knowing I've already seen heaven
But for now,
I guess I'm just lucky to be here.

'fire & ice'

It should never get to the point
Where screaming becomes the only
Way to get your attention.
Where breaking glass onto
Hard wood floors is the only way
To prove I still care.
I want to fall asleep every night
Knowing you're still going to
Want to kiss me in the morning.
Because diving into question marks
Makes the air in my lungs
Feel like knives trying to dance
Against my rib cage.
And swimming in the dark waters
Of doubts make me go blind.
So, I'd rather send you small whispers
In the middle of the night and
Let them fall across your skin,
And I'd rather fill shot glasses to the brim
And toast to us being young, crazy, and happy.
And I'd rather fall asleep with my lips igniting
At the thought of waking up next to you.
Because you are fire, and I am ice.
Wanting nothing more than to melt with you
Forever.

'*blurred lines*'

We spent
Hours, minutes, seconds
Memorizing each other's details.
Tracing the outlines
Of your tattoos,
Spilling our darkest secrets
Upon white pillows.
Getting tangled within laughter and
Cotton threads on warm afternoons
And now
I can't even remember
Which side of the bed you slept on.
Isn't that crazy?
How something that was once so magnified
Can become so blurred.

'daydreams'

The things I remember about you
Show up in the clouds.
I turn my head back and forth trying to figure out
Which parts of you I'm searching for.
Is it your secret smile?
The one you would give in the mornings
When no one but me was looking?
Could it be I'm searching for
Someone that doesn't exist?
I replay those mornings over and over
And only come up with the secrets
You smiled away.
And maybe if I had been looking harder
I would've been able to see the things you were hiding.
If I hadn't had my head in the clouds then,
I wouldn't be searching for you in them now.

'turquatic'

Let him pick out my perfume
So I can forever be
His favorite scent.
Kiss his tattoo's
While leaking stanzas
Of poetry into his skin.
Adorn his lips
With lyrics written
In Egyptian silk
Mirrors above the bed
Because it's beautiful
To watch.
Place soft whispers
Against his neck
Caressing his name
In high notes
Make music jealous.
Falsetto's echo
Against ecstasy laced walls.
It's always better high.
Writing love sonnets
On fogged windows.
Mimicking sculptures,
Passion screaming out of my pores,
And when it's all over
When our breathing slows
I watch him close his eyes
And listen to him inhale
The scent he chose.

And at first it was fun.
The days blurring together
With weed smoke.
The delicate desserts.
The night's spent
With laughter wrapped around
A deadly kind of love.
And I wanted to believe in it.
I wanted it to be real
But there was a darkness I tried to avoid.
The secrets spilled into the
Middle of my lap
Learning things, I didn't know existed.
Fleeing the scene of what
I thought was the end
Of everything we had become.
And that night I made you promise.
A promise that, even now
Through the insanity
And the confusion
And the heartache
It's a promise I would never
Break.

I like you.
Because your story has
Jagged edges, kinda like mine.
And despite your
Sloppy cursive
I don't mind scrolling
Through your wrinkled pages
Because your past is beautiful.
Even though the haunted details
You're made of are sometimes
Hidden by muted words.
Twisted tongues covered in verbs,
But I heard you.
Your story is honest and unfiltered.
Question marks live
At the end of all your sentences
Kinda like mine do.
I like you.
Because happily ever after's
Have never made their way
Into your chapters.
And you have pages missing.
Torn from those who have
Tried to break your spine.
But I have a few to spare.
We can share them if you'd like.
Or you can kiss me
Till our lips go numb.
I promise I won't mind
The paper cuts on my tongue.

You were dangerous
I know.
I saw the signs but
Chose to ignore
Because love alone
Has almost killed me.
Twice.

But I figured
Risking my heart with you
Was worth it
Anyways and absolutely.

'patronus charm'

It takes an act of disappearance
To make the trick complete.
Don't believe in what you can't see
'till the white rabbit and the top hat meet.
I've been staring at old photos
Smoking to Kendrick, watching the lighter flicker.
Drunk off my mistakes and dark liquor.
Magicians and poets
Have always been soulmates.
We are written in the same ink.
We think the same way.
Spellbound and hell bound.
On the edge, ready to plunge
Into the depths of gone too far,
Prepared to die among
Abracadabra's gone wrong.
This could have been a love song.
Would've called it Hocus Pocus.
Because your magic had ill motives
And my words could never hold us.
Somewhere we lost our focus
Please don't start looking for me now.
I'm not hidden behind a curtain.
I'm taking a hiatus from us.
When I'll be back,
Is not for certain.

'*911*'

I was standing there naked.
And I don't know why.
Just standing there.
And I don't know how I got there.
And sirens were blaring outside.
The blue and red lights flashing
Creating purple shadows on my cheeks.
I think I was surrendering.
I wasn't holding a white flag
But I had my hands above my head.
I can't remember what I had done.
Is having too many thoughts a crime?
Maybe I fell in love too many times.
I don't know.
But I was out of breath.
And exhausted.
With bloodied ankles and a weak mind.
And all I wanted to do
Was to go home.

We become accustomed to accustoms.
Blankly following the paths of
Bad habits formed in a matter of seconds.
Days begin to repeat themselves and
Soon we're stuck walking in a circle,
Spinning ourselves dizzy.
Is this when we become insane?
Carving initials into yesterday's
Tree hoping to look back and remember
Who we once were.
Losing our name to inconsistent promises
And knowing there is nothing left of
Ourselves to break; so the glass falls and
The pieces scatter across the floor of our sanity.

How do you explain that you are putting together an
invisible puzzle?

'haunted'

There was a house I once died in.
My name is written in cursive on the walls.
My whisper echoes through the halls.
Listen closely.
There is a secret in that house.
A secret I didn't know was there,
But I felt it everywhere.
Its teeth sinking into my neck,
The venom trying to take my last breath.
But it wasn't the secret that killed me.
It was the truth that did.
And knowing what I know...

I may be haunted for many lifetimes to come.

'somewhere in a dream'

Beach sand makes its way into your pockets.
And you haven't been to the beach in weeks.
You check the bottom of your shoes for remnants of sea salt.
You shower with summer air hitting your skin,
And believe you're there.
You believe you're reading Langston Hughes on a blanket,
With the deferring sun blazing,
In an oversized t-shirt, drinking sparking water
You pour out of an indigo bottle.
The waves wash away all of the doubts.
All of the fear.
All of the noise.
You eat mangos and let the juice trickle down your chin.
It's perfect.
Close your eyes.
You're here now.
Even if it's just a memory.

He lies to her, so he can lie to me.
What truth does he ever speak?
He doesn't because the truth
Might break his teeth.
So he resorts to breaking hearts
So his twisted tongue
Has a place to sleep.

I guess without that smile
He's as broken as
The tears I weep.

'*Those who live in glass houses should not throw stones*'

I had a house once.
And in that house there were *things*.
Things with memories encrypted onto them.
There were chairs we sat and laughed in.
All the photographs, I adored you.
Books we never read.
Walls with too many words unsaid.
I never wanted to leave.
Too afraid of what I might find,
What secrets you kept under your sleeve.
I sound proofed our bedroom so you did not hear
Me scream when I found *her scent* underneath
Your pillow.
The hearts on the window from fogged mornings.
Mornings I could not sleep from the nights you
Pretended to love me.
Stained red lipstick smeared across buttoned shirts;
A cliché I ignored every time.
and every time,
You would return to me with
A little less than what you left with.
The warnings were deafening but I covered my ears
With your hands and begged you to make
The sirens stop, and you would kiss my cheek
Just as innocently as I would sweep away
Her footprints in the doorway.
The wine bottles spilled every time you left;
Drinking to the nights alone, in our bed.
This house became a knife and I bled when you fled.
Cutting deeper, the nights longer, the mornings colder,
Wrapping myself in our bedsheets.
Wondering how it was you could hold her, when you had me.
Sadly, our happy home became a
Vacant hole and I walked the halls of what was.
The broken chairs, the crooked pictures, the shattered dreams.
This is what our love had become.

I sold that house to a woman who didn't mind the mess.
She said nothing could compare to the tangles in her chest.
When she stepped into the doorway,
I could almost hear her heart break.
Her scent was familiar.
Her red lipstick blared.
She pushed my hand away when I went to give her the key.
Opened her purse and pulled out her own.
I smiled and left that house.

And I built myself a home.

'just let go'

You will never be able to grasp
What has already fled.
You cannot hang on
To knotted thread.
Every name has a taste.
Every scent has a body.
The senses never lie
And the truth is always haunting.
The outlines of what used to be
Are engraved in your palms
And you can't stop looking at your hands.
Forever retracing the men
Who have touched and left.
But please don't get lost
In what could have been.
You are a fly to a spider
In those tangled webs.
Be here.
Be now.
Do not cry into pools of memories
That never happened.
You will drown.

You love hard.

So you make excuses for him

Because it's passion when he says

Not to call him tonight.

Because it's romantic when he calls

At 2am.

You love hard.

So you put up with his lies,

Like you're doing him a favor.

You love hard.

So you don't question his mind games

And you don't question his motives.

Mostly because he told you

Not to ask questions.

But you love hard though.

And when it's good

It's so good.

Good enough to settle for.

Good enough to go back on your word

That you weren't going back.

Good enough to fuck and never make love.

Good enough to stop speaking to your family.

Good enough to forget your morals.

Good enough to tell your friends

It ain't that bad.

When it is.

It is

So

Much

Worse.

'Love shouldn't be so hard.'

'haunted II'

This house is haunted by your memory.
These bones are shattered by your touch.
These veins are poisoned by your kiss.
They said I went missing.
They said they found me in a nightmare.
I woke up screaming.
Your name burned into my skin.

I will not be ashamed to admit that I am afraid.
Bravery is showing up, despite those fears.
I'm here.
I'm scared.
But I'm here.

'the unanswered questions'

There are pieces of myself
That are still in your possession.
How did you do it?
How did you get away with all of my secrets?
Unscathed.
Untouched.
You appear on the faces of strangers saying hello,
Knowing what you know,
Leaving me as a ghost.
How do you do that?
Steal all of my secrets and then
Blame it on me?

After we broke up, I woke up
From the dream that kept
Reality from me.
I saw the man
I wanted you to be.
But my nightmares have been truer
Than you ever were.
A blur of fairy tales undone,
A mirage of images captured
In small frames.
I blame you for the insomnia.
Dark circles around my eyes remind me
Of the times where
Your name was tangled in
Hushed lullabies that sang me to sleep.
A fantasy built upon
Cloud 9 and serendipity.
Falsely letting me fall deeper
Into a dream that wasn't meant for me.
And you left memories that
Made me believe in
Make believe.
But fairy tales do not exist
And though we kissed
Once upon a time
I am woke enough to know
That you were never
Real.

We didn't make it this time around.
Our past selves are somewhere laughing at us.
Maybe we tried to late.
Maybe we lied and missed fate.
Maybe we broke it too many times.
I don't know but
I can still feel you thinking about me.
So in the next lifetime,
Keep that same energy.

'soulmates'

'of the fittest'

You are not allowed to love me
Until you know all my secrets.
You are not allowed to love me
Until you survive them.

So maybe I've been looking for you
In places maybe, I shouldn't be.
Leaving clues that I know
Only you could follow.
Revisiting memories in the hopes
Of finding you standing there,
Wanting to relive the moments
Just as bad as me.
Wanting to taste the innocence one last time.
To remember what it feels like to be free.
Maybe I've been looking for you,
Hoping you've been looking for me.

'babygirl'

He
Purposely
Stole your soul
Without consequence
Which incidentally
Led to the death
Of your common sense
Degraded yourself
When his methods
Became too complex
Over powered your mind set
So you had to settle for less
And babygirl

You ain't been the same ever since.

Your memory is a blade.

I find myself bleeding blue.

And it's your eyes that never seem to fade.

And it's those mornings that never seemed too early.

And it's those nights that never seemed to end.

Kings never die.

I should have known that.

Your voice is a ghost.

A skeleton in my closet

I thought I had buried.

You were supposed to turn to dust.

Instead you became the sand

In-between my toes on beaches

We once laughed on.

I don't remember the joke now

But I do remember wondering what this would feel like.

The blade of your memory

Against my fingertips.

Wondering who was going

To kill who

First.

Because the worst way to kill someone is to
tell them you love them
and not mean it.

three.

'I hope you still browse my pages, even after you've read all
of the words.

-*Jill Scott*

This is where the change happens.
When you least expect it.
When the world is still sleeping.
But you are awake.
Moving in silence.
Keeping a promise to yourself.
The change happens here.
The difference between then and now.
You will never be who you were before, after this.
Let that be the reason you never look back.
It's happening.
You're changing.
And it's beautiful.

I am all the darkness
And I am all the light.
I am the grey line served
On a silver platter.
I am the pair of emerald eyes,
That were always too blind.
I can't see close. And I can't see far.
But I saw you.
I reside where you do not.
But you are everywhere.
I can fly and swim, and yet
I do not move.
I am everything and nothing.
I am everywhere and nowhere.
I am bruised,
But I am healing.

I am you. And you are me.
And we are lovely.

When the heart break settles and
The stiffness of the drink from last night
Wears off,
You'll wake up in a bed
Built only for you,
In sheets that no longer
Carry the scent of
Lovers who left.
You will wake up
Knowing you love you more
Than anyone ever could.

And it will be enough.

'message'

I am going to leave this here to tell you that
I know how it feels to not know how you're feeling.
And I know how it feels to feel too much.
I also know how it feels to not know the difference.
I also know that sometimes, there just isn't one.
I am leaving this here to tell you
That's okay.

Do not waste time on people who don't value yours.

'forgiveness'

Forgive yourself beloved.
Forgive the parts of you that are still broken.
Forgive yourself for having faith.
For believing in something or someone.
Forgive your past.
Forgive yourself for not having it all figured out.
Forgive yourself for making the same mistakes.
Forgive yourself for wanting space.
Forgive the words you never said.
Forgive the words you didn't mean.
Forgive yourself for wanting more.
Forgiveness is a luxury.
And you have always been royal.
Forgive yourself for ever thinking otherwise.

The people who hurt you the most
Teach you the most.
Pay attention.

Keep going.
Even when it seems like everyone is ahead.
Even when you feel like you'll never catch up.
Keep going.
You'll get there.

I don't have the time to match everyone's energy.
I can only stay true to who I am and if that doesn't vibe with you,
then I wish you well.

But you are not welcome here.

Showing someone who
You really are takes courage.
Appreciate the bravery
In their honesty.
You never know
How many battles
They had to fight
Just to show you.

These are the lessons I had to learn.
All the love poems I had to write.
I had to fight with the idea that
I am enough.
I kept turning myself into a
Home with no windows and locked doors.
I didn't realize I was a castle.
I didn't know then that I was housing
Enough space to grow cities.
To build galaxies.
These are all the lessons that taught me
I am more than a body.
I am a soul.

People *outgrow* each other all the time and it's okay.
Some things just don't fit anymore.

'for the dreamers'

It is easy to say
I hope all your dreams come true.
But real life is hard.
So instead I will say
I hope you have the strength
To wake up every single day
And work your ass off.
I pray that if you fail
You have the courage to try again.
I wish nothing but positivity to
Enter your thoughts.
I pray for your creativity,
For your inspiration,
For your ambition and your determination.
I hope you never lose sight of your dreams
Because when life gets hard
It's easy to forget.
And as far as hoping they come true, well
That goes without saying.

Watch your words.
Don't become heavy with things
You say and don't mean.
You will drown before you
Say the things you meant
To the people you want
To say them to.

Being tough all the time is tough sometimes.

'anxiety'

You wince at a papercut.
You try and shake off the sting but
It stays with you all day.
The annoying burn you can't make go away.

No pain is too small.
If it hurts,

It just hurts.

I am doing my best and I don't care what that looks like to you.

I do not want to feel the same way
I felt today, tomorrow.
Because the day washed over me,
Leaving traces of doubt in tiny footsteps.
I wasn't sure if I had stopped breathing or if
There was simply no more air left.
There was a knot tied in the pit of my stomach
Where butterflies used to flutter.
My head too filled with chaos and clutter.
Today was the kind of day that lasts lifetimes.
But tomorrow will be here soon.
And I will wake up
Brand new.

You are not made of glass.
How dare you walk with whispers.
Like you are not a bullet.
Like you are not made of metal.
How absurd to tip toe on eggshells
When you are an atomic bomb.
Fragile things break
Into pieces that scatter.
But you are not made of glass,
You are not meant to shatter.

Some moments are just meant to be lived. But then there are others that are meant to be devoured.

'an oxymoron walks into a bar'

'It would be awfully good to be a fine mess with you.
Look at me; I've broken into
A cold sweat just at the sight of you.
I'm almost exactly sure
That you are the oxymoron I've been
Searching my whole life for.
Did you come here alone?'

'?!'

'Well then,
Let's be alone, together'.

If the love you give isn't matched
By the love you receive
Then quite frankly darling,
It's a love you don't need.

'love letter to a whirlwind'

You curse under your breath
Thinking no one can hear you.
But the world is tuned in.
There is so much more to life
Than being angry at it.
You have been hanging onto fairy tales
That are shaped like suicides
Around your neck.
Hardly hanging on by a thread.
You blame other women
For the voices inside your head,
For the perfumes that you don't use
Found on your lover's bed.
You are beautiful, but you are broken.
Twisted into knots by men who
Pinky promised their way into
Your fragile palms.
They never held on long enough.
You sleep next to ghosts
Who will never know your favorite color
Or your middle name.
You blame your mother
For not teaching you how to be strong.
You have been to hell and back
And you are still not impressed.
Constantly trying to find new ways to break yourself
To prove that you can be healed.
You are beautiful, but you are lost.
Hoping that there is someone [anyone]
Out there looking for you.
But darling,
No one can catch you
If you keep running.

The world owes you nothing.
Stay kind.
Be humble.
Have respect.

It's always comes back when it's pure.

'reminder: stay true'

I don't know where your hurt comes from
But I want to hold your hand
While you heal.

'brick by brick'

It took years to rebuild.
A broken masterpiece.
Fallen and shattered.
But I did it.
Brick by brick.
Built myself from the ground up.
And now
I'm stronger than ever.

'dear god, make me a bird so I can fly far, far away from here'

I had a prayer like Jenny's once.
I think everyone wishes for wings when they're young.
Innocence lost on swollen tongues,
Smiles hung backwards,
Happily ever after's falling short
Of prince charming's.
Impurity being stained into dirtied hands.
I was 15 when he told me I wasn't pretty enough.
And somehow those words became
The soundtrack that my insecurities
Used to dance to.
I'd weep prayers into my pillows.
Folding my skin back trying to find roses.
I had to stop wishing and praying.
I had to learn that I had thorns too.
I had to realize that I was born with wings.
And once I did
I flew.

It's simple.
All she wants is
A good man to be good to
And if that's asking for too much
Then you are simply
Not good enough for her.

My heart breaks for you.
Tears run down my face when
The world fights against you.
Because I know how heavy that weight is.
I know how dark it can get.
But I need you to believe in galaxies.
The darkness is not your enemy.
I need you to believe in those shadowed blankets
And wrap yourself in them.
Be the night sky.
Be the stars.
And shine.

Recount all the times
You said, 'never mind'.
Those are the words you need to say.
Those are the words they need to hear.

These are only words.

Script from a twisted wrist.

A hand that's been kissed.

Words flowing from burnt fingertips.

These are just words.

Being swallowed and ignored.

Words, evaporating into blank eyes

That don't love me anymore.

Numb tongues wrapping around moonlit sighs.

Inhaled the love and exhaled metaphoric lies.

Watch them rise through cracked throats

And break in midair like neglected smoke

These are just words.

The ones I never spoke.

'friends'

Thankful for the ones that have stayed.
Grateful for the ones that have left.
Love for those I chose to leave behind.

I had a conversation with the universe.
She told me exactly what I needed to hear,
Exactly when I needed to hear it.

I met up with Karma the other day.
She told me to stop worrying so much,
That she had everything under control.

Patience called to tell me that
The wait would be worth it
And then he put me on hold.

Humility came out of nowhere
And tripped me in the middle of the street,
Kissed me on the cheek and then ran.

I couldn't even be mad.
I ran into Cupid yesterday
And he thanked me for not giving up hope,
I thanked him for not giving up on me.

Forgiveness knew I didn't want to see her,
But she showed up anyways
Practically forcing herself in.
I'm glad she did.
I've never felt lighter.

And today
I sat in silence
Completely humbled and filled with love
And whispered the words thank you
A million times.

I am running so I don't feel as lost.
Running.
Into whirlwinds and mountains.
Lands where
God rests his hands, somewhere.
Shoulders do not touch here.
I am running deeper and harder.
Faster than my feet can carry.
I am not the feather I thought I was,
And my heart is heavy with burdens.
Running
To forget that I was once
Still.
I am unmoved by these events
And though I could shed a thousand
Tears, my cheeks remain dry
And the desert surrounds my eyes.
I can see the wind blowing.
I can taste the memories.
Floating gently around my fingertips.
Stop.
I want to remember this moment
Catching my breath.
No, I have to keep going.
I am running to savor these moments.
Stretching my soul across plains
And valley's
And islands.
Hugging the world with both arms.
Running
Running
Running
Till I see that these mountains
Are not as still as I thought they were.

In those small moments
Of wanting to go back,
Even if just for a small taste.
Tell yourself you are not who you were.
There is nothing for you there.
Do not make up apologies you never received.
Remind yourself it was never love.
Do not get caught up in what you thought you knew
When you know better.
And even if they try to give you a reason to stay
Even if it tastes good.
Throw it away and keep going.
You deserve
Exquisite.

four.

'All water has a perfect memory and is forever trying to
get back to where it was.'
Toni Morrison

'the history of me'

I stripped it of all the poetry.
Took away the inspiration and the sadness.
Ripped off the band aids and the madness.
I took a dive and swam in every scar.
I had to get back to the beginning.
Traced it like tattoos on skin.
I had to watch it play backwards
To understand what it all meant.
I left it on until it was nothing but static.
I broke every bone and every promise.
I dug up ever skeleton buried in my closet.
And there I was.
Back to where I started.
I woke up in a dream, remembering a past me.
Falling in love all over.
Dancing in my brilliance.
Look at what I survived!
And the most beautiful part
Is knowing that I would
The entire time.

'the elevator kiss'

Because it was 5am.

And we were still exhausted.

The excitement of the night before still heavy on our tongues.

There was electricity as we moved.

Even though the sun was still asleep.

We walked in silence,

And even muted, *our love was loud*.

We waited and laughed about something small.

And then suddenly the elevator became our own world.

A foreign universe and only we existed.

This is where you kissed me.

And it was supposed to a kiss that was short and quick.

It was supposed to be insignificant.

But it was different.

It was urgent. It was important. It was necessary.

And I felt it everywhere.

Maybe it was the way you were looking at me.

Maybe it was the way your neck curved.

Maybe it was because it felt like our lips were magnets.

Maybe it's the fact that it was 5am in an elevator.

And maybe I'm trying to make it more romantic than it was.

Every kiss from you is a worthy one but this specific kiss had a purpose.

This one had a mission.

This one needed a poem.

Because I felt it everywhere.

And had an earthquake erupted at the same moment,

I wouldn't have noticed.

'lets go'

I'm down to jump in a car with you
And just go.
Without maps, without a destination.
Just you, me and an open road.
I am so down to put the music on shuffle
And not touch it for hours.
And when that one song comes on
[and there is always that one song]
We'll look at each other with wide eyes
And dance uncontrollably and then
Years later I'll look at you
And mouth the words
And you'll just get it
And it will be so good.
I'm definitely down for conversations at 4am,
Underneath starlit blankets,
About religion, and hip hop and poetry
And how we don't really see the difference between them.
I am so down to explore the crevasses of
Your mind and spend my time
Falling in love with all your secrets.
I am so down for hand holding
And slow dancing, and bold love and romancing.
And sweet texts, and great sex and
Love letters unfolding.
And the not knowing and the maybe's
And not caring cause we're crazy.
I am so down for an adventure with you.
Pack your heart, I'll pack mine.
Get in the car,
We're going.

I brought a few things, so bear with me.
I will put all my thoughts in your palms.
And all my fears on your back.
If it's okay, I'm going to tuck my memories.
Behind your ears so when you hear me crying
You won't be afraid.
I am going to hang all my photographs
On your smile.
That way they will never be crooked.
I know I come with a lot of baggage.
But there are truths I cannot hide and
Sometimes I just need someone to confide in.
So can I put my nightmares on your chest?
Can I rest my childhood insecurities on your wrists
The same way they are written on mine?
If I kiss my secrets onto your lips, will you tell them?
Because right now I need a sanctuary.
I need protection.
Tonight, I need your mouth to be a lighthouse.
Tonight, I need you to be my home.
Let me sleep here.
Let me stay.
Please.
Let me live here.
Maybe for a night.
Maybe forever.

'bad habits'

I know you are not them.
You tell me to quit biting my nails
The same way you tell me to stop
Comparing you to
The men I've loved before.
I know.
But some habits are just really hard to break.

'a poem for long distance relationships'

There are three things
That I know for sure.
You are not here,
I am not there,
And trying to
Turn that into poetry
Is fucking torture.

'the battlefield'

I should tell you now
That you are entering a war zone,
And I pray that you've packed your armor.
I should tell you
That I have broken pieces
Laying around everywhere
And they cut deep.
But only if you let them.
You should know that I have been loved before.
Good and bad.
Which means I know how to appreciate a good man
And how to discard of an unworthy one.
I'm only telling you this
Because I know you hate surprises and I want
You to be fully prepared for the ghosts
That live in my closet.
I'm haunted by a past that is terrifying and
Beautiful at the same time.
I should tell you now
That loving me is dangerous.
And if you decide to stay
Then my darling,
You deserve a medal for your bravery

I know it seems like
I'm not listening.
But I get lost out here.
And sometimes it's hard
To separate your voice
From the ones living inside my head.
And when I'm quiet, please understand
There are sirens singing through my pillows.
But somehow you always find me.
Your voice is the one that brings me home.
I hear you.
I'm on my way.
Thank you for not screaming.

'all the crazy'

The muses that have occupied my pages
Have all thought the same as you.
So, no, you're not crazy.
I take to paper, my wounds, my joys,
My inner secrets exposed by prose.
And it can be sweet.
The words will stick to you like caramel.
You will love to be embellished in between
Pretty words.
Feel adored in metaphors.
But it can be brutal.
Because, like me, you are not perfect.
And if you ask them, my muses might
Show you their bruises and tell you
That you're crazy to love me.
But their chapters have closed,
Where ours has just begun.
And I can't say that I
Won't write with weapons
Or that I won't try to
Shut you out when I get scared.
But I can promise to be gentle if
You promise to not think I'm crazy.

There was a time that I felt winter in July.
Thank you for bringing Summer back to me.

'120213'

We don't have much time
And the stars don't look like this in the city.
So, I need you to love me now and here.
Without restraint or fear.
Make me forget that tomorrow
Will be filled with only memories.
Your kiss has to last lifetimes
Because the lifelines on my palms
Are not long enough, and it's unfair.
So, lets create our own forever
Write a classic on the pages of our sheets
Paint a masterpiece upon my skin
Sink into the deepest parts of me.
This will be our history.
So, love me now.
Because the stars have never looked as
Beautiful as they do when I look at you and
Making love has never tasted this good.

I am now
Unapologetically unavailable.
I was in reach for years.
And still you never asked
How I was doing.
Never had to look for
What was right in front of you.
But I've been moving.
And my days are hurried.
So, I've buried you in a place
Where I had too much time.
Where I confused infatuation with boredom.
I no longer have the luxury of lazy love.
I am busy.
And if you're not going to come through
With a sense of urgency,
Then you're already too late.

I'm not a mind reader, love.
Can't always know what you're thinking.
But I promise to listen up
When your heart is speaking.

'the pieces of us'

I am failing you.
And I can feel it
Swelling in the air.
And sometimes
I think that I think too much.
Too in my head.
But it lingers, like dust.
Crawling into our bed
Leaving the sheets cold and lifeless.
I miss you, but I don't know how to tell you.
I love you, but I don't know how to show you.
I want to fix this, but
I can't remember what it was
That broke first.

You are failing me.
And I know you can feel it
In the absence of my sweetness.
Words have turned into weapons.
And I know I do not fight fair.
But I think you think too much.
And you drink to forget.
Leaving the echo of whiskey in our bed.
I watch you when you sleep.
And I wish you would come back.
Because I miss you, but you don't miss me.
Because I love you, but you don't see.
Because we could fix this,
All we need to do is
Pick up the first piece.

'mantra'

Learning patience and trusting the process.
Living in the moment and finding peace within myself.
Letting go of the past and holding onto my dreams.
And never forgetting that I'm worth all of it.

'zhuri's dreams'

I want to live up here.
In the skies, with the stars.
I want my daughter to be unafraid of mars.
There is a broken city down there,
With blood on the streets.
Tears for water and fangs for teeth.
How can I bring a child into those wars?
How do I prepare her for what's in store?
No, I'll stay up here and lay her head
On a cloud.
Where her dreams can fly far,
Instead of below where they
Drown.

'1013'

A year ago
I wasn't so alone.
I had you.
In the palms of my hands.
They're so vacant now.
Only these words to hold.
I miss you.
I do.
Every single day.
It's been a year.
I'm so sorry.

'*engaged*'

I am mad.
At myself for letting this happen.
For letting myself even question it.
Embarrassed, really.
But you see a diamond, and realize
There's a void.
You see a sped-up version
Of what you thought you had
And realize a few years have gone by
Without even noticing.
I can admit
That a hint of jealously shames my left hand.
But you put on a smile,
And the happiness is pure
And you take the pictures,
Because that's what friends do.
And then you go home.
And you wrap your arms around a love
You know is real and rare to find.
And hope that you're not somehow
Getting left behind.

You're holding the key, free yourself.

'a prayer of gratitude'

Let me fall asleep
To the sound of the wind
Telling the leaves
Goodnight stories.
Allow my heavy exhales to be
Swallowed by
Sweet tomorrow's
With the promise of
An easier inhale.
Might God sing me
A lullaby tonight and
Rock me away
To a heaven like dream.
May my heart be healed
By the kiss of the autumn breeze
And by the delicacy of the moon's smile.
And if permitted
Allow me to awake with dry eyes
And a happy soul,
Filled with gratitude,
Wanting to give nothing more or less
Than all the love I have left.

I just want to be special to someone. I want to be something that someone can't live without. I want to be air. To someone.

The blast took away half of your soul.
I watched you crumble to the ground,
Chanting prayers into your past.
With the sounds of nuclear weapons in the distance,
We began reminiscing on the nights where silence
Cradled our dreams as we slept.
We believed in them once.
Leaving trails of tears on heartbroken walkways,
We began marching to two different tunes,
Counting full moons,
Forgetting who we were.
And now, with these sirens
And memories getting lost in gun smoke,
And broken promises swelling
Underneath bullet proof vests
All I wish is to be captured by
Your silent sighs and to held by your twisted smile,
And for all the dreams
You used to hold so tightly during the bombings
To come true.

'closes eyes'

'woman with words II'

She reminds me of the girl from San Francisco.
The one I didn't have to worry about. He swore.
The one he loved when he didn't want to love me anymore.
He let that girl break my heart.
She reminds me of nights I spent driving myself insane.
Pouring over details I didn't have
Hoping to find an answer to the questions I couldn't ask.
She reminds me of a summer I once lost.
I remember feeling so stuck
With him making me feel crazy as fuck
For feeling what I felt.
I spent that year chasing the sun.
So don't tell me to calm down.
Because I have been here before.
And right now
I'm 19, with no boundaries and no regrets.
Ready to end it all.
She reminds me of the insecurities
I convinced myself I had outgrown.
I guess it's not that simple.
I guess I thought that since time had passed
So did these triggers.
I guess even when you think you've moved on,
The trauma of a past love still lingers.
She shows up with black hair and black eyes
Haunting me.
Making a mockery of my love for you.
And it makes me feel as small as it did then.
I blame you the same way I blamed him.

It's comes down to the words, right?
The ones she says to you and the ones you say to me.
This is a war between the truth
And what I want to believe.

'the rooftop party'

I could never forget it.
I remember, I said
'Who is that?'
Because I recognized your energy
From a lifetime before.
And then somehow
I ended up on a rooftop
Celebrating you
On accident.
And years later I was singing for you.
And years after that, I was crying over you.
And a lifetime later here I am,
Reminiscing
About
You.

'just kids'

We still make out on the couch
Like teenagers.
Sloppy and juvenile.
With childlike passion.
We still giggle under the sheets.
Play hide & go seek.
And tag.
You been it.
Since forever.
I hope we never
Outgrow this love.

Your kiss is a question
I want to spend the rest of my life
Trying to solve.

Your name follows me in the wind.

I can taste it in the clear waters.

I dance in your melodies.

I have wrapped myself in your memory

More times than I can count.

You have sung me to sing sleep on my darkest nights.

I am sun kissed from the warmth of your soul.

You are never too far.

I carry you everywhere I go.

'island ting'

We're oceans apart.
I've been putting seashells up to my ears
And I can't hear you anymore.
Drowning in the sandcastles
We once built by the shore.
But this is life.
And sometimes it takes
Getting lost in the deep in
To really learn how to swim.
And now waves no longer scare me.
And I'm racing against every current,
Picking up the pieces I left
Stranded on your beach.
It was beautiful,
But I live on an island now.

Your memory plays over and over in my head like my favorite love songs.

'come back'

Every time you go
Everything gets a little
Blurry.
It's not that I can't live without you.
I could.
I just don't want to.
So everything kind of spirals,
Because you keep me grounded.
And when you leave
I count down the minutes
Until you'll be back
To keep my world intact.

'ode to the past'

Sometimes my past escapes me
Like a foreign thing.
It almost feels like a dream.
A memory from a life that wasn't mine.
It's like everything before this
Was just me watching someone else.
And sometimes I can feel the pain in my chest
And swear it doesn't belong to me.
Because surely no one could have survived
So many bullet wounds.
Surely no one could have made it out of the darkness
Blinded by heartbreak.
Surely.
But when I fall asleep
Filled to the brim with joy
Next to a love that I love so dearly,
I close my eyes and run to that little girl I used to be
And whisper,
'it happened but you're okay now and everything is so
beautiful.
I am so proud of you'

'magic hands'

It lingers every time.
Sits, patient and placid.
The echo branded into my skin.
I think your hands are made of magic.
They hold on to pieces of myself
That I thought I had destroyed.
An innocence I had long forgotten.
You come back to me every time.
And I am reminded of all the things
I could never say out loud.
The things I want to say, but I'm not allowed.
Begging to be forgiven,
I go to war with the world for you.
Every time.
And I show up with scars and bloodied knuckles.
Running from the memory, in a panic.
You bring me back every time.
You and those hands
Made of magic.

'tracy chapman complex'

Caught a vibe just looking at you.
You make me feel invincible.
Which is wild since
You used to make me feel invisible.
I don't trust myself around your energy.
It's too much to handle.
You told me that once.
Said I was too much.
And now we're in this space of
Being strangers and being in love.
I don't know how it happened.
On a roof.
In a groove.
High in the kitchen.
I couldn't move.
Your hands on my waist,
I called it love, the irony.
Because you called it something else entirely.
And now I'm too many glasses in to deny the fire in me.
Tell me that is what you see.
Tell me you've thought about breaking laws to find me.
Tell me when you look at the stars, it's my name you hear.
Tell me it's my face you see at the end of the day.
I swear I will never leave,
Just give me one reason to stay.

I've fallen in love so hard
That my rib cage has broken.
And not because
He didn't catch me when I fell,
But because my heart literally
Exploded out of it
When he did.

Pain has never felt so good.

*Words do not complicate things. It's the fact that we're too
afraid to say them, that does.
But you deserve to relieve those burdens.
You deserve to be heard.
Always.*

*And it's not the questions that will make you crazy.
It's the fear of asking them that will.
But you deserve peace of mind.
You deserve answers.
Always.*

To be held by you
The way lungs hold air,
Is all I really need
To survive.

Find what brings you peace
And stay there for as
Long as you can.

'*perfection*'

Let's be honest.
You're not perfect, either.
Even the strongest man gets
His heart broken.
Even the most beautiful woman
Pinches at her flaws.
So, if you think that you are
Alone in this, you're not.
Because let's be honest.
Being human is about making mistakes anyways.
And it's an absurd concept to think
No one else knows what it's like
To feel defeated or broken.
To feel like we are somehow fighting
Against everyone except ourselves.
To feel like avoiding mirrors is a genius idea
So we can continue to point broken fingers
At a world that has us blindfolded.
A world that has us so convinced
That failing is worse than trying.
Aren't you tired of being lied to?
Life fucking hurts sometimes
And it's okay to say that out loud.
And you don't have to proud
Of your scars, but you shouldn't
Have to hide them either.
And bad days are necessary,
Stop being ashamed of them.
I'm just saying.
Perfection is idolized as heavily as
The painted faced behind these filtered screens.
Did you forget we're human beings?
Find some humility.
Find some truth.
Because let's be honest,
Your story isn't as pretty
As you try to sell it.
Just tell it.

I've been writing these words instead of hearing them.
Flowers cannot grow without water.
I need to tend to my own garden.

'blooming'

'the lighthouse'

I saw a lighthouse in the distance.
Convinced myself that if I could just swim
Past the ocean of tears that
Had consumed my heaviest years,
I'd be able to fill the voids
That all those broken promises had
Left me with.
If I could just get through the misery,
I'd remember what it felt like to love.
And be loved.
And that was enough for me to unleash
The fists my hands had created.
It was enough for me break through the
Chains that love's harsh reality had
Kept me in.
It was enough to make me let go of my pride,
For me to believe
In what was on the other side.
I dove into those dirty waters,
Fully aware of the skeletons
Waiting for me at the bottom.
Knowing that there were secrets
I was not ready to face yet.
And realities that I had kept quiet.
I plummeted to the deep end,
Abandoning the shallow waters
That I had carefully
Kept at bay.
And so the story goes, the first cut is always the deepest,
And I bled for the man who left
My heart stranded.
There it was, suffering and confused
Wondering where he went.
He found a new ocean.
I found my forgotten youth down there.
Cold and shivering,
Holding its breath,
With bloodied wrists and

Remorseful eyes.
And I found my mother's tears.
Her strength carrying her fears.
It was dark here.
And I could feel the wrath of
Regret swarming around me
And all I wanted to do was form
A new army,
But I was a lone soldier
Fighting against painful memories
That my heart possessed.
I found broken pieces of emerald gems,
That seemed to burn when I touched them.
I didn't rest.
Bled through the pain,
The sharp needles of words unsaid
Pulled at my heart strings,
Creating heartbroken melodies.
This is where I found my sister.
I wanted to run to her.
I wanted to hear her sing.
But the music suffered.
So I cried.
And I could feel my brother's hand
Trying to hold onto any type of hope
We had left.
I watched my father's face disappear into the blue depths
Of abandonment.
Refusing to ask for forgiveness.
It broke my heart again.
And the glass of yesterday's window
Was shattered, and nothing mattered
But the lighthouse that would save me.
And maybe save us.
I trusted that it held the cure
For heartbreak.
The glue to piece together unfulfilled dreams,
The thread to sew back humanity's ripped seams.
Because it seems we are broken,
When really, we are just exhausted

From swimming in these oceans.
When I finally came to,
After catching my breath
After almost drowning in sorrow,
I looked up and realized
I had not moved.
Bruised and confused
My theories remained unproved.
But before I had the chance to
Blame the heavens for my misfortune,
I looked down and saw the
Unlocked chains.
I was free.
And in the distance, the lighthouse was still beaming
And it was the most beautiful mirage
I had ever seen.

I have written a million letters.
A million times.
A million different ways.
I have given my soul to these words
With the hope they make it into your hands.
With the hope that they reach you,
Finally returning home.
I hope you let them stay.
Please put them on a bookshelf,
I've said all I needed to say.

Love,

Tiana Monique

P.S. Write me back.

Made in the USA
Monee, IL
17 November 2020

48117789R00094